COUNTY DURHAM & NORTHUMBERLAND

Edited By Jess Giaffreda

First published in Great Britain in 2018 by:

 Young**Writers**

Young Writers
Remus House
Coltsfoot Drive
Peterborough
PE2 9BF
Telephone: 01733 890066
Website: www.youngwriters.co.uk

FOREWORD

Young Writers was created in 1991 with the express purpose of promoting and encouraging creative writing. Each competition we create is tailored to the relevant age group, hopefully giving each child the inspiration and incentive to create their own piece of writing, whether it's a poem or a short story. We truly believe that seeing it in print gives pupils a sense of achievement and pride in their work and themselves.

Our latest competition, Monster Poetry, focuses on uncovering the different techniques used in poetry and encouraging pupils to explore new ways to write a poem. Using a mix of imagination, expression and poetic styles, this anthology is an impressive snapshot of the inventive, original and skilful writing of young people today. These poems showcase the creativity and talent of these budding new writers as they learn the skills of writing, and we hope you are as entertained by them as we are.

CONTENTS

Ringway Primary School, Choppington

Joe Harvey (7)	63
Reese Emily Barron (8)	64
Isaac Wilson (8)	66
Lucas Matthew Murray (8)	68
Millie Dickson (8)	69
Keane Harrison (8)	70
Isla Grace Dawson (8)	71
Sophie Turnbull (7)	72
Medina Grace Tate (8)	73
Jack Thomas Lockhart (8)	74
Abbie-Mae Dixon (8)	75
Maezy Rae (7)	76
Sophie Heather Moira Gibbinson (8)	77

St Cuthbert's RC First School, Tweedmouth

Mhairi McLeman (9)	78
Macey Brooke Anderson (9)	80
Edvinas Smilgys	81
Caelin Hannah Farish	82
Clara Henriques (7)	83
Mabel Skelly	84
Leo Gray (8)	85
Lexie Brooke Clark	86
Miley Wood (8)	87

St Patrick's Roman Catholic Primary School, Langley Moor

Jessica Elizabeth Thompson (9)	88
Leo Currien (9)	89
Joanna Bull (9)	90
Harris Armstrong (9)	91
Ella Ellies (7)	92
Belladouna Pulotu (8)	93
Cassidy Philip Di Lella Edwards (9)	94
Izabel Alex Bartlett (8)	95
Kelsey Oakes (7)	96
Robert Ellison (8)	97

Ian Kenny (8)	98
Vaidotas Treciokas (8)	99

Whitehouse Primary School, Elm Tree

Martha McGrother (8)	100
Talia Anne Lowe (9)	102
James Angus Macdonald (9)	104
Josie Mae Jolly (9)	106
Amy Louise Metcalf (8)	107
Elizabeth Dalgleish (8)	108
Elif Tiffany (9)	110
Joey Saysell (7)	112
Hakeem Khan (8)	113
Joseph Canvin-Reid (8)	114
Alice Potter (9)	115
Mohammedadeen Yousaf (9)	116
Jack Lewis Dunham (9)	117
Maggie May George (9)	118
Poppi-Lei Brooks (9)	119
Hollie Brennan (9)	120
Amy May Jackson (9)	121
Jack Dalzell (8)	122
Millie Rafferty (9)	123
Elias Sturman (9)	124
Lillia Grace Tucker (9)	125
Ruby Atkinson (8)	126
Elena Rurzman (9)	127
Connie Manning (9)	128
Isobel Southall (9)	129
Taylor Camilleri (9)	130
Daniel Harris (9)	131
Elliott Godfrey (9)	132
Freja Carlsson (8)	133
JJ Hardy (9)	134
Jake Cinnamond (8)	135
Chelsea Shipman (8)	136
Matthew Longfield (9)	137
Eleanor Lowe (8)	138
James Wood (8)	139
Matthew Teague (9)	140
Tegan Henry (8)	141
Poppy McEwan (8)	142

THE POEMS

Where Is Your Gosh?

Born from an experiment gone wrong,
Blasted into the heavens when the lab blew up
Gosh and his brother landed on the window of 3
Wilby Close
Gosh went lurking through the house at night,
He caused shivers of terror down the kids' spines
His hairy, brown legs allowing him to stomp down,
The long, dark landing of the house
His mouth gaping as his head lolled on his
shoulders
Gosh's eyes stared past the oak bathroom door,
He wasn't aiming for anywhere
He liked striking fear into people's hearts
Do you hear something outside your door?
Perhaps it could be your own Gosh, waiting?

Imogen Ullock (11)
Bedlington Station Primary School, Bedlington

The Smug

Smug

A black substance that looks like tar, dribbling down its eerie eyes
Its head floats, violet blobs are between them like disfigured plums
As spine-chilling as a shadow moving towards you
As unsettling as a horror movie
A pair of scarlet horns that are as crimson as bubbling lava
An angel's hoop glows golden around the horns making you blind
As black as coal, it makes you cower in fear

Smug

A whiff of this thing makes you vomit
A pile of disgusting rubbish getting worse by the second
As smelly as a pile of disturbing corpses that have been left for months

Smug

A terrifying scratch on your door is Smug carving
to get in just like a tiger wanting food
It's just a tiger wanting food
A mean, stray cat ready to pounce and bite
A starving, wild dog ready to eat you.

Smug.

Autumn Pomfret (9)

Howden Le Wear Primary School, Howden Le Wear

Deezo

Deezo
Deezo is my best monster
He comes from Canada where snow falls as fast as
cars
He is as friendly as a playful Dalmatian puppy
chasing a ball
As placid as a ginger kitten sleeping on a furry mat
Deezo

Deezo
Spotty like cherries scattered on the bright grass
The fur is freezing snow with large footprints on it
Eyes are round tennis balls
The fur is as soft as a teddy bear getting cuddled
at night
Horns are super swords in battle
Deezo

Deezo
A smell as sweet as honey,
Some delicious candyfloss at the fabulous fair
Deezo

Deezo
As silent as golden honey in a giant jar,
His bark is as loud as a car horn
Deezo!

Rachel Jones (10)

Howden Le Wear Primary School, Howden Le Wear

Zaboot

As hairy as a furry yeti,
As spiky as a sharp dagger,
Enchanted by a magic sorcerer,
Zaboot
As curious as chemistry,
As cross as a moody hedgehog,
Imagine a calculator and times it by ten,
That's its brain power,
Zaboot
As disgusting as broccoli,
As whiffy as an unemptied bin,
Someone who hasn't bathed for a year,
Doesn't smell half as bad as him,
Zaboot
As gruff as a goat with a sore throat,
As loud as a bongo drum,
On an angry meter, he would be off the scale!

Nathan Webster (9)
Howden Le Wear Primary School, Howden Le Wear

The Monster

Monster,
As red as a blazing fire,
As red as a cherry tomato in a bowl of veg,
Yellow and orange teeth like daggers trying to eat you,
Its nose is like a pig's,
A body as round as a beach ball,
Its legs as black as the street cat roaming around the garbage,
Its arms are twigs,
Its eyes are fried eggs but yellow and pink,
A spotty Dalmatian,
Its body is like a carpet,
Its nails are like witches,
Antennae, long, black and round,
Eyes as wide as an owl's,

Monster.

Chloe Demeyre (10)
Howden Le Wear Primary School, Howden Le Wear

My Monster

As yellow as a zap of lightning on a stormy night,
As big as a secondary school,
As rancid as a garbage can,
As shiny as a bright star in the midnight sky,
As sacred as a sparkling blue sapphire,
Its eyes are as sharp as a knight's blade,
As dangerous as a zombie outbreak,
Its shriek is as high-pitched as a newborn baby,
As annoying as a tweeting bird in the early
morning,
Its tail is as rigid as a rusty saw blade,
As fast as a tiger hunting its prey,

Monster.

Lucas Carswell (10)
Howden Le Wear Primary School, Howden Le Wear

My Monster

Monster,
As yellow as a banana on a giant plant,
As fluffy as a fancy poodle,
A smoky pile of dust,
Monster,
As kind as a beautiful butterfly,
As loyal as a cute dog,
As curious as chemistry,
A protective tiger with its cubs,
Monster,
As scented as perfume,
As sweet-smelling as drizzly, melted chocolate,
A daisy trapped in claws
Monster,
As noisy as a gorilla,
A pigeon in the morning waking you up,
Monster!

Holly Featonby (9)
Howden Le Wear Primary School, Howden Le Wear

The Monster

Monster,

As hairy as an extremely fluffy pom-pom floating
inside of a balloon,
As short as a cute, little guinea pig, running around
in its beige cage,
As round as a light blue bubble bouncing in the
breeze,
As white as crystal snow waiting to be melted into
water,
As loud as a lonely lion in the zoo,
As smelly as misty smoke floating in a burnt down
house,
As nasty as a vicious werewolf roaming around on
a dark, dim night

Monster.

Toby Joesph Gardiner (10)
Howden Le Wear Primary School, Howden Le Wear

The Monster

Monster,
As orange as a flaming fire in front of my eyes,
As dangerous as a fifty foot drop onto spikes,
As mean as a vicious dog on a night,
As smelly as a rotting corpse on a haunted night,
As scary as a maggoty zombie you might see on TV,
As cunning as a slithery snake in the jungle,
As cold as an icy freezer,
As scaly as a massive fish in the ocean,
As tall as the Eiffel Tower on a summer's day,
Monster.

Huw Halliley (10)
Howden Le Wear Primary School, Howden Le Wear

The Dickelnock

Dickelnock,
As unpleasant as warm peanut soup,
As rapid as an angry cheetah on the go,
When it comes to eating delicious people, he never says no,
Dickelnock

Dickelnock
As rotten as a pineapple chucked out two-and-a-half years ago,
As smelly as a toxic bottle of rum,
As blue as the midday sky,
As vast as a pyramid in the middle of Egypt,
Dickelnock.

Fearne Abbott (9)
Howden Le Wear Primary School, Howden Le Wear

Zing The Monster

Zing,

As dotty as a newborn Dalmatian,
Spots as shiny red as rubies at night,
Teeth as sharp as megalodon's front teeth,
Horns as sharp as a bull,
Hair as fiery as a forest fire,

Voice as soft as a lamb,
Footsteps as calm as a Sunday school night,

Zing,

As friendly as a super cute puppy chasing its tail,
Zing.

Rhys Lowes (10)
Howden Le Wear Primary School, Howden Le Wear

The Monster

Monster

As friendly as a playful puppy trying to catch his colourful frisbee
As happy as a child playing on a bouncy castle on a hot summer's day
As lively as a dog chasing a cat

Monster

As smelly as a fragranced flower growing in the smelly fields
As smelly as strong mint growing in the vast, green bushes

Monster.

Megan Johnson (10)
Howden Le Wear Primary School, Howden Le Wear

The Monster

Monster
As black as the midnight sky
As vicious as a shark eating a boat
Fangs as sharp as daggers

Monster

Body as armoured as a German tank,
As loud as a cranky crane lifting a car
As green as grass on a hot summer's day
As enormous as Tilted Towers

Monster.

Cameron James Kell (10)
Howden Le Wear Primary School, Howden Le Wear

The Endy

Endy,

As spotty as a playful Dalmatian
As furry as a cute kitten
Teeth as round and huge as rabbits
Its eyes are caterpillars laid out on a thin branch

Endy,

As friendly as a butterfly flying peacefully
As huggable as a teddy
It's a giant, soft plushie

Endy.

Robyn Jean Alison Donegan (9)
Howden Le Wear Primary School, Howden Le Wear

16

The Killer Machine

The Killer Machine
As violent as the Devil,
As armoured as a tank
As vicious as a Titanoboa

The Killer Machine
As greasy as oil,
As patchy as an old jacket

The Killer Machine
As smelly as an air freshener,
As thin as a medium stick

The Killer Machine.

Joe Mekatoa (10)
Howden Le Wear Primary School, Howden Le Wear

The Monster

Monster,

As crazy as a cheeky, little monkey,
As friendly as a tiny puppy,
As bouncy as a trampoline with crazy springs,
As colourful as a bright rainbow sitting in the sky,
As stinky as a pink pig stomping around in muck,
As hairy as the giant bigfoot monster,

Monster.

Lewis Wood (9)
Howden Le Wear Primary School, Howden Le Wear

The Monster

Monster,

As purple as juicy grapes sat in the fruit bowl
Eyes as wide as a wise owl
As spotty as a Dalmatian
Tongue as floppy as a puppy's
Arms as thin as sticks
Eyes as yellow as golden honey
As spotty as chickenpox
As vicious as an angry shark

Monster.

Teegan Maria Adamson (10)
Howden Le Wear Primary School, Howden Le Wear

The Monster

Monster,

Eyes as stretched as tights,
A body as green as grass,
Orange eyes as big as baubles

Monster,
Monster,

A bright, pink tongue like flip-flops
White, clean teeth like diamonds,
Wrinkles like old people

Monster,
Monster.

Scarlett Rose Shield (9)
Howden Le Wear Primary School, Howden Le Wear

The Monster

Monster

As grouchy as an old man
As slimy as honey
As beaming as the boiling sun
As spotty as a Dalmatian
As royal as the Queen
As dirty as a pig
As round as an egg, freshly laid

Monster.

Thomas Wright Pickles (10)
Howden Le Wear Primary School, Howden Le Wear

The Monster

Monster,
As friendly as a playful puppy,
She smells as delightful as marmalade in a jar,
She is as round as a hard-boiled egg,
As spiky as needles on a Christmas tree,
Her voice is as deep as a killer whale.

Finley Hall (9)
Howden Le Wear Primary School, Howden Le Wear

My Monster

Monster

As dark as an alleyway in the midnight sky
As mysterious as Area 51,
As deadly as a level 1000 mega Mewtwo
Horns as terrifying as the monster under your bed

Monster.

Charlie Gilloway (10)
Howden Le Wear Primary School, Howden Le Wear

Pete The Pretty Monster

Pete was very pretty,
And he had a little, white kitty
But Pete was very picky,
He never ate like a piggy

One sunny day,
He wanted to have a picnic
Along the giant, beautiful river,
Where lots of kids play

He packed some food,
He packed some drinks
Grabbed his car keys,
And went in his fancy car for a long drive

There were lots of kids there,
And some adults too
But they were all dirty,
So Pretty Pete was very angry
So he put dresses on them with flower crowns too

Pretty Pete was happy,
He had the whole river

Everyone left but
At least everyone was pretty.

Ava Moralee (10)

Mowbray Primary School, Guide Post

Sweet Munching Monster

In a tree, in the sky,
Yellow sunlight beams down,
The monster munches chocolate bars,
Jumping down from the trees,
Whacking his tail,
Flying in the sky,
He has three legs but never begs,
Running around,
His name is 3Horncon
Running around, stealing sweets
His friends are having fun, now don't be dull
Don't be dull, we will sing a song
He likes to run, he runs 1000 mph
You will never see him
His hair is curly so don't be afraid
He likes to eat sweets so don't be sorry
This monster likes to sing and also likes to wear bling.

Georgia Cowell (9)
Mowbray Primary School, Guide Post

The Rose Gold Monster

One big, rose gold monster
Woke up in a dark, damp cave.

It was a risk to meet her
She had large teeth
Her name was Tiarly
She lived in a dark, damp cave.

She only came out at night
She was very clever
She lived in a dark, damp cave.

She moved so slow
But that was fine
She was very attractive
She was hard to see at night.

Tiarly was her name
It was hard to tell
But she was very clever and fluffy
And she lived in a dark, damp cave.

Iona J Cowell (9)
Mowbray Primary School, Guide Post

Mischievous Monster

I was looking underground for diamonds
And I saw a monster!
It looked like a boy
I walked towards him
And he said,
"Hello!"
I could tell he was funny straight away
I asked him what his name was
He replied,
"Steven."
He looked kind
He said, "I've got no friends,
Can you be mine?"
"Yes," I said
And we live together
We're happy
It's the best thing that's happened to me
In my life.

Elise Ann Acar (8)
Mowbray Primary School, Guide Post

The Mean Monster

Under your bed,
There lurking
Is a body and a head,
Watch for Baldy Bob

His body is black,
His horns are red
There he is, under your bed,
Watch for Baldy Bob

He is furious and angry,
Don't be on his bad side
He persuades you with candy,
Watch for Baldy Bob

His four eyes are scary,
So are his four legs and arms
His body is really hairy,
Watch for Baldy Bob.

Lacey Traba (9)
Mowbray Primary School, Guide Post

The Undiscovered Monster

A broken-down vehicle
A vast monster comes out from hiding
Precious is her name
Pretty, pink and large teeth she has
Really a risk
But intelligent she is
Excitable and clumsy
They are her things
But together, they can be dangerous
She is plump
But that's a good thing
Isn't it?
Undiscovered she is
Sometimes happy
Friendly and brave as well
Fluffy as can be.

Isla Davidson (9)
Mowbray Primary School, Guide Post

Wolf Air The Flying Wolf

In the janitor's closet,
In Mowbray Primary School,
Just don't make a sound,
Or fool around,
You might get a fright,
Because the closet isn't bright.

The monster is called Wolf Air,
It has a lot of hair,
He sings in the shower,
He scrubs with a flower,
When it is night,
It isn't so bright,
When he eats bones,
He sometimes has them with cones.

Paige Greaves (9)
Mowbray Primary School, Guide Post

A Day In The Life Of Luminous Fred

He lives on a shipwreck far, far away
Further than a plane

Frightening, ferocious and you can get scared of
his teeth

Luminous and bright,
You can see him in your sight

He's slimy and gooey,
And you can feel it

Hairy, furry and you can feel his furry fur
He's disgusting, mouldy and you can taste him
He eats metal and drinks sewage water.

Ewan Grey (10)
Mowbray Primary School, Guide Post

Monster Poem

In an underground mansion
Lies a ferocious monster
Who is sucking on blood
His name is Scorwing Slime
He is a cheeky rainbow slime monster
He has twenty legs and never begs.

His monster friends are having a blast
He isn't the last
He is a rapid runner
He has a scorpion tail
He always wails
He is a mighty beast
Who always likes to feast.

Olivia Beadnell (9)
Mowbray Primary School, Guide Post

Darling Devil

In a burrow underground,
Lives a gentle monster,
Evil but gentle,
Named Darling Devil,
This frightful monster loves to sing,
And wears a bit of bling,
To see this monster you must be a bat,
For he loves to sleep,
When the sun is high,
He loves to play with the other guys,
Plus he eats a lot of flies,
Eating veg he carefully settles,
Whilst eating nettles.

Daisy Ella Carr (9)
Mowbray Primary School, Guide Post

Beamox The Banshee

Beamox the booming banshee screams all day
long,
However, its screams are fatal
To those who may hear its screams,
Watch out, they can kill you

It's as big as can be,
Also very hairy all over its body

This flesh-eating monster may look cute,
But it is very vicious
Don't ever go near it,
If you do, don't say I didn't warn you!

Thomas Routledge (10)
Mowbray Primary School, Guide Post

The Weird Monster

On a cloud in the air,
Lies a pink beast,
Having a feast
Of mice and rats.

Only wears a top,
That says, *mop mop mop,*
He is called Tiana
And does not like llamas.

He is very, very ugly
And not that snuggly,
He is very skinny
And not that mini.

He is very snotty
And he doesn't like mopping.

Samii Leightley (8)
Mowbray Primary School, Guide Post

The Monster That Ate Everyone

In the trenches,
There is a crocodile-shaped newt,
It is eating its intimidating friend,
At the breathtaking base, don't interfere,
It will eat you even though you are his type.
Try not to touch it
It smells of vomiting humans
And it will gobble you up in a heartbeat.
At the creepy cabin,
The monster still stays
To slay humans!

Mick Hardy (9)
Mowbray Primary School, Guide Post

The Unusual, Smelly Monster

An unusual, smelly monster
Who lived in a small dustbin
Was a trivial orange monster,
With a smile and a pair of sharp teeth

He had one giant eye,
Three long legs
Arms that could stretch,
And two painted horns

He was a small, vicious monster,
Climbing in his bin
Eating all he could,
And sleeping all the time.

Amy Elliott (10)
Mowbray Primary School, Guide Post

Monster Poem

In a log cave,
There is a dandelion-teeth monster with backward
fur
You might think it's mean
But think first, it's kind!

Here is a secret,
He's got a girlfriend who is pink.

Here is a secret,
He's got a big black tongue.

He has got green lips,
Yuck!

It's got a box for a head.

Amanda Louise Griffin Price (8)
Mowbray Primary School, Guide Post

Monsters

There's a monster,
He's invading the city.

There's a monster,
Stealing all of the people's food.

There's a monster,
Destroying vehicles.

There's a monster,
Roaming around.

There's a monster,
Squishing people.

There's a monster,
Burning the city.

Dyllan Cawley (8)
Mowbray Primary School, Guide Post

In A Log Cave

In a log cave,
There is a terrifying monster
There is a grape-coloured monster
In a log cave,
And he has got four eyeballs,
And rose eyelashes
He has got a pink girlfriend,
And a box head
He drinks horse blood,
And he has black nails,
And turquoise lips
Sharp, scary horns,
And purple pricks.

Tiarli Miller (8)
Mowbray Primary School, Guide Post

The Good Monster

There is a monster
who is kind,
who helps children,
and has good, curly horns.

It speaks English
and changes colour,
and helps people who
are being bothered.

It has hair
but not as much as a bear.
It's clean and spotless
and eats chocolate éclairs.

Jared Gordon (8)
Mowbray Primary School, Guide Post

The Devil

A dark, dreary cave
Bear blood everywhere
Don't go near him or you could get possessed
You could be a crisp
You could get stabbed by his horns
I guess you can call him a devil
He likes video games
He throws you up and you get stabbed with spikes
He can rip your face with his fire tail.

Liam Davison (8)
Mowbray Primary School, Guide Post

The Monster

Once there lived a monster
Oh, ever so tall
After all, he did live in a hole
He was covered in green, sticky slime
He ate slugs in mugs
His life was perfect
He never got caught drinking from the moat
Oh, how rude
He was never in the mood
He had warts all around his face!

Imogen Coyle (8)
Mowbray Primary School, Guide Post

The Multi Creature

In the swamp lies a beast
That eats teeth and meat from the butcher's
Ever so hairy, he's very scary
He has different eyes, you could faint
Very slimy nose, lots of spikes
Lots of floppy legs
Sharp teeth, better watch out
He could kill you in flash
Sharp ears as well!

Jamie Chard (7)
Mowbray Primary School, Guide Post

The Mischief Monster

I went to a cave and I saw a monster
He was fluffy and cute but he didn't have any manners
He was kind and helpful and small
He had horns but they weren't that long
He had brown eyes, a black tongue and was blue
I walked towards him and he shouted, "Hello!"

Keira Davidson (7)
Mowbray Primary School, Guide Post

The Pleasant Monster

In a cave,
Lives the monster,
Who eats mice,
And has two legs and one arm.

Who's playing with his human friends,
Having fun,
To see this monster, you must be awake,
For you only see him once a day.

Kasey Taylor (9)
Mowbray Primary School, Guide Post

Monster

It has got scary fins,
It loves to eat spicy food
It's got scary, red eyes
It does not like glitter
It hates Halloween and Christmas
It likes to jump around
Its house is spooky,
It loves chocolate.

Amelia Rose Davidson (7)
Mowbray Primary School, Guide Post

The Horrible Monster

The monster
The huge monster
The huge, fat monster
The huge, fat, scary monster
The huge, fat, scary, ugly monster
The huge, fat, scary, ugly, angry monster.

Ella Louise Adams (9)
Mowbray Primary School, Guide Post

Skittle Monster

Next to a rainbow,
Lies a hairy monster,
And people chop him with a chainsaw.
He uses his horn to make corn,
He poos Skittles,
When he pittles.

Corey Davison (8)
Mowbray Primary School, Guide Post

The Bonga Banger Boo

On the Bonga Banger Boo,
all the monster go *achoo*
but over all of the hills,
lives a monster who kills.
On the Bonga Banger Bing,
all the trees ping
and all the monsters from before
disappear with one blow.
One big, hairy mess has teeth a little less
sharp than a single pick,
its hair could impale you worse than a stick.
With a huge, powerful jaw,
you'll be scared with just one roar.
A roar louder than a lion, louder than a bang,
this hideous beast shouldn't exist, to say the least.
This spotty, messed up thing eats food in a *ding*.
On the Bonga Banger Boo,
all the monster go *achoo*
but over all of the hills,
lives a monster who kills.

Miaya McCulla (9)
Pelton Community Primary School, Pelton

A Monster Dream!

My monster's from Love Land
He's friendly and sweet
He lives in a cave
And has lots to eat.

One day in the summer
We went to the beach
Had a big BBQ
And ate lots of meat.

On the way home
I called out his name
He turned and he laughed
As we played our game.

After a long fun-filled day
We both felt complete
So we got tucked up in bed
And fell fast asleep.

I woke up with a jump
A shout and a scream

A suddenly realised
It was all just a dream.

Ella Mckitten (7)

Pelton Community Primary School, Pelton

The Mythical Creature

The mythical creature was waiting for a special
feast
No one was scarier than this beast
Under the darkness of the night
Watch out, you might have got a fright!
His eyes were as bright as a spark
And his eyes glowed in the dark
You might have wanted to put him in a trap
You might have wanted to run a lap
After he came
It was such a shame
He was good and he learnt his lesson
But he sent somebody a blessing
And then he was friends with everybody
And he will never have a lonely body.

Jodi Layton (8)
Pelton Community Primary School, Pelton

The Wibbly Wobble Mr Shuffler Comes To Town

My arm's stretching out like blossom on a tree,
Mr Shuffler, Mr Shuffler

My eyes are as wide as an owls in the dark,
Mr Shuffler, Mr Shuffler

My antennae stretch out like ropes on a trapeze,
Mr Shuffler, Mr Shuffler

My body floats around like a ship at sea on a
windy day,
Mr Shuffler, Mr Shuffler

My nose is as curly as a curly French fry,
Mr Shuffler, Mr Shuffler

My hands are as soft as a petal from the flower,
Mr Shuffler, Mr Shuffler.

Grace Otto (9)
Pelton Community Primary School, Pelton

Fluffy

My name is Fluffy,
My fur is so puffy.
I come from deep space,
I will always greet you with a happy face.
My home planet, Rainbow, is bright,
The three suns reflect a lot of light.
I like to help others,
I'll be there for your grandmother.
I follow the latest trends,
We could be the best of friends.
I donate to charity,
My best feature is clarity.
I'm on this planet to help and to share love,
I hope I won't be judged, as I come from above!

Jennifer Louise Brinkworth (8)
Pelton Community Primary School, Pelton

Harley And The Dainty Secret

Harley was a normal boy
He loved to play with all his toys
But then one day he heard a bash
Then he heard a mighty bang
He felt different, he didn't deny
Was he a monster with four eyes?
This was a question he would like to solve
Why was he a monster, big and strong?
He was green and furry with eleven legs so long
He had ninety-nine arms that had patches on.

Jessica Moffat (7)
Pelton Community Primary School, Pelton

Lightning Flame

Lightning Flame
In the way
Says hello
To you and me.

Lightning Flame
In the way
Says hi to your friends
Another day.

Lightning Flame
In the way
When you play
In the day.

Lightning Flame
Is off, away
To the sweet shop,
Hooray!

Lightning Flame
Says bye

And buys the sweets
Hooray!

"Ha, ha, ha
Lots of sweets for me
Yum, yum
In my tummy!"

Liam Wright (9)
Pelton Community Primary School, Pelton

The Monster At The Bottom Of The Garden

M y monster sits at the bottom of the garden

O n the trees, he sits all day eating midges

N o one goes in the back garden, his dumping ground it is

S o if you go in the back garden, you will need a shower

T ried Air Wick air freshener, but it won't work

E ric the cat is missing

R ocky the dog has disappeared.

Abigail Louise Martin (8)

Pelton Community Primary School, Pelton

Big Bill And Jelly Jill

There once was a monster called Big Bill,
He had a best friend called Jelly Jill,
They always had fun,
In the sun,
They watched the dolphins play,
All day, every day,
Until the day turned into night,
Oh, what a sight,
To see the stars,
Absolutely no cars,
Big Bill and Jelly Jill,
Friends forever and ever,
Until the very, very end.

Abby Maxwell (10)

Pelton Community Primary School, Pelton

My Nightmare

Lewis is a monster who comes during the night.
When I see him I close my eyes really tight.
Sometimes I wake up and I turn on the light.
Sometimes I don't and get a big fright.
I told my friends and they laughed at me
But then they saw a giant bee and they believe
It was Lewis after all!

Leah Young (11)

Pelton Community Primary School, Pelton

Mersadania Madness

This beast has shark tails,
And she has ugly scabs
The sand thing has emerald skin,
On Fortnite, she only has one win

Laser beam eyes that can soar,
She will also hurt the core
She absolutely loves funny David,
And she's never isolated

She's as sad as a storm of rain,
She's nearly killed Liam Payne
Her green Rapunzel hair can strangle a great
white,
Even blue whales get a fright!

She would love to be a sinister Pokémon,
How about wicked Soloman?
Her face's shadow is frightening,
And she never gets struck by lightning.

Joe Harvey (7)
Ringway Primary School, Choppington

Zuzu The Monster

Meet Zuzu the monster,
She likes to do fixing
And her favourite celebrity is Alesha Dixon

Zuzu is really greedy,
Naughty and mean
Other monsters say she's bossy,
And she thinks she's the queen

She's orange and spotty,
She plants lots of nettles
When she has chickenpox, she's really dotty,
Why can't she just plant petals?

She has orange skin,
And she wears a tutu
She eats out the bin
In my opinion, I think she's cuckoo!

She has five eyes,
Her favourite food is French fries
She nearly caused a shipwreck,
And she killed Ant and Dec!

Zuzu has lots of hissy fits,
She doesn't eat her tea,
And she acts like Honey G!

Reese Emily Barron (8)
Ringway Primary School, Choppington

Snot The Shape-Shifting Dog

One day, Snot was walking in the street,
Whilst the sun was bringing the heat
All his friends were walking with him,
When a dog was looking grim
They like to sing whilst they walk,
Or maybe talk
Although he is a pug,
He always wants a hug
Snot likes to say, "Hi!"
All he eats is sausage pie,
He likes to play sports,
All his house is made of quartz
Snot has three friends who are named,
Hissy, Cheetos and Pringles
They always have mosquitoes,
Both his friends live in a dog house mansion,
They've been in a police station
Some strangers say, "Trust us!"

His friends dance with him,
Some strangers glare with grim.

Isaac Wilson (8)
Ringway Primary School, Choppington

Graff The Earth Dragon

Graff the Earth dragon is a dragon from the planet X7,
And his age is over eleven
He has emerald talons,
And Griffin-like horns
And in fact, his favourite food is prawns!
He was tired of living on a cloud,
Also, he felt very proud

One day, he left his cloud on his own adventure,
He went into the Milky Way
He came to a planet,
And everybody made him pay!
He saw a boy,
And he said, "Ahoy!"
The boy took him to his house,
He said to him, "I love to play the Wii!"
The Earth dragon said, "I don't know if he likes me."

Lucas Matthew Murray (8)
Ringway Primary School, Choppington

Fluffy Phoeby

Fluffy Phoeby is cute,
And her favourite food is fruit
She is naughty,
And really sporty

Where she lives is really nice,
And one of her friends is made out of rice
There is a colourful rainbow,
And a tadpole

She gives lots of gifts,
And I fell off a cliff
She is really silly,
Like Millie and her friend, Billy

Every time she goes on an aeroplane,
She does not have a brain
Every time she plays a game,
She needs her first name

She is really funny,
When she acts like a bunny.

Millie Dickson (8)
Ringway Primary School, Choppington

Sparky The Electro Dragon

Sparky the electro dragon,
Is that colossal he's bigger than the largest
Volkswagen
In BC555, he was born in a volcano,
A minute later, there was a tornado

When he was fifteen, he saved the world,
I said, "Where do you come from, I guess the
underworld?"
His middle name is T,
And he totally acts like Honey G

When he's round the bend,
I played FIFA with the mode end to end
When I played Pokémon Go,
He said, "My favourite Pokémon is the water type
Popplio."

Keane Harrison (8)
Ringway Primary School, Choppington

The Poem About Pretty Paris

Whilst Pretty Paris walks through the city of Paris,
On a day of May
Her skin is as clean and as fresh as glass,
And at night, her blue eyes glow

Pretty Paris is as pretty as a kitty,
She is talented
Her friend, Kate Hate, does not like rotten apples

Pretty Paris always eats dinner at a fancy restaurant,
She always has fun with her friends
Lindsay Liar loves to lie about pie,
Mermaid Mia likes to swim at the gym,
Cupcake Cora loves to eat cake whilst she takes a shower.

Isla Grace Dawson (8)
Ringway Primary School, Choppington

Starsy The Dragon

Meet Starsy the dragon,
She carries a wagon
In the wagon are some sweets,
She loves beats

She has pink skin,
And she eats from a bin
She lives in a volcano,
When she's asleep, there's a tornado

In her family, she's the queen,
She's always clean
She wears a blue bow,
And she's from Planet Mo-Mo.

Sophie Turnbull (7)
Ringway Primary School, Choppington

Monster Fuzzypants

Meet Mr Fuzzypants,
If she eats lots of pasta, she will get faster
And her eyes are like fresh-cut grass,
She is as heavy as a yeti,
And she is very happy.

Her fur is like an orange,
And she has friends
She likes to play a lot with her friends
They will always be friends,
Until the end
Her teeth are as sharp as a shark's.

Medina Grace Tate (8)
Ringway Primary School, Choppington

Hissy The Hydra

Hissy the Hydra is evil,
She likes wolves
She is medieval,
She is friends with a werewolf

She walked through the forest one day,
She likes people for a meal
Hissy was doing maths with an array,
She loves maths!

Hissy plays Fortnite all day,
On her Xbox all the time
Before night,
Then she turns the Xbox off.

Jack Thomas Lockhart (8)
Ringway Primary School, Choppington

Dirty Dave

In the deep sink,
There is a wimp,
His name is Dirty Dave

He is really naughty,
The worst thing is, he likes his bogies,
He likes to play all day

He has got a wife,
She is all white,
Her name is Susan,
When she is having a snooze,
Dirty Dave is on the booze.

Abbie-Mae Dixon (8)
Ringway Primary School, Choppington

Meet Doughnut Head Cop

When Doughnut Head Cop, she pops,
She even wears eight socks!
She is slimy and limey,
She is purple and pink,
And she never stinks.

She winks and blinks,
When I opened the fridge door,
I fell on the floor.

Maezy Rae (7)
Ringway Primary School, Choppington

Rainbow Monster

Rainbow Monster under the sea, she is free
She lives in Sea Shell Palace, and she is called Alice
She keeps the sea clean and she's mean
Rainbow Monster has rainbow fur,
And her friend, Alice, is always next to her.

Sophie Heather Moira Gibbinson (8)
Ringway Primary School, Choppington

Katie The Kind Monster

K atie the kind monster

A very helpful monster

T his super secret agent

I f she was ever seen

E veryone would think she was just a rock!

T here was a very lazy boy called Tiy

H e threw a lot of rubber away

E very single day

K ind Katie decided, "I must do something about it!"

I nvisible Katie sneaked into Tiy's garden

"N ow," said Katie, "what should I do about this?

D oes Tiy go to bed at nine?"

M onster Katie got all of the rubbish he threw in a big, black bag

O ver into Tiy's house

N obody noticed her

S ilently, she tipped the bag of rubbish into his garden

T iy woke up when Katie had gone and found the rubbish

E veryone helped clear it up

R emembering about this problem, every time Tiy
was going to drop something!

Mhairi McLeman (9)
St Cuthbert's RC First School, Tweedmouth

Monster Poem

M oney Monster sitting quietly

O n top of the large rock

N obody knew he was near the cave

S uddenly, he heard a noise getting louder and louder

T errified, he slid off the rock

E ventually, the noise stopped and

R unning towards him was Alice

F riendly, kind Alice

R an to the cave

"I hope she wants a friend

E verybody needs a friend," said Money

N o one wanted to be lonely

D ancing around being friends.

Macey Brooke Anderson (9)
St Cuthbert's RC First School, Tweedmouth

Laboratory Monster

A monster is a secret laboratory,
That is four times bigger than a full grown yeti,
And a hundred times stronger than a T-rex!

The eyes that make you go in the opposite
direction,
And the fangs of a gigantic wolf

The huge monster and hungry monster,
Is much smarter than the smartest human on
Earth,
And more agile than an alpha wolf

Faster than a peregrine falcon,
It has blood-red eyes that glow in the pitch black,
To help it see in the dark.

Edvinas Smilgys
St Cuthbert's RC First School, Tweedmouth

The Creepy Cheetah

There is a monster,
She has sharp claws,
Wings with spiders on them,
A furry tail,
Fuzzy paws
And sharp teeth

She is called Chrystal
When the moon comes out,
She is the meanest
She is as black as the night sky,
As she hunts her prey

She lives in a dark, gloomy castle,
In a town called Creepsville
Her servants are witches
Watch out, because she will get you!

Caelin Hannah Farish
St Cuthbert's RC First School, Tweedmouth

Odd, Spotty Monster

M onster Harry is spotty, blue and purple

O nly Harry has spots, he is the odd one out

N o, he is not tall, but he has five beady eyes

S ilently, baby Harry has fallen asleep

T iny, tickly fingers in his mouth

E very time someone walks down the street, he watches

R eady to make friends. Would you like to be his friend?

Clara Henriques (7)

St Cuthbert's RC First School, Tweedmouth

Mystical Monsters

M ystical monsters live under your feet,

O nly some are very scary

N o one is as nasty as Laim

S harp fangs as pointy as a knife

T iny ears that can hear from miles away

E very day, he listens to your footsteps from underneath the ground

R eally nasty Laim is always watching you!

Mabel Skelly
St Cuthbert's RC First School, Tweedmouth

Monster

M ost monsters live in a big, dark cave

O n a mountain to see their prey

N ot humans, only fish, cows, pigs and birds

S cary nights are coming, so much more food!

T all monsters are sprinting in creepy nights

E normous cows, yum yum!

R un cow, run! I want to eat you!

Leo Gray (8)
St Cuthbert's RC First School, Tweedmouth

Mystical Monster

There was a monster called Shaggy
With purple spikes on his back
And covered in spiders
He has a witch for a servant
And an eagle for a pet
In the night, he turns as black as the sky
And sleeps under the carpet
Below the floorboards,
Shaggy is the scariest monster.

Lexie Brooke Clark
St Cuthbert's RC First School, Tweedmouth

How Elly Began!

M oving in the distance
O n a land of wonder
N o one knew what it was
S cared was the thing
T all but frightened
E ven friendly
R ather weird.

Miley Wood (8)

St Cuthbert's RC First School, Tweedmouth

Vectoris, The Baddest Of Them All!

Vectoris is the almighty monster in your town,
When he is angry, he has a face of a frown
He is as quick as the Flash,
His all-time favourite dinner is mash
His secret home is under the sea,
Warning, he's always there having a cup of tea

He dances all night long,
And he also sings his favourite song
"La la da, la la di!" he sings,
Shhh, another secret - he has wings!
His eyes glow as bright as the sun,
Although he is really dumb

His body is a fluffball,
But he had to spoil it by breaking one law
When he saw a snake,
He then chucked it in a lake

Everyone calls him 'Fast Fox',
The worst thing he leaves is his diseased socks!

Jessica Elizabeth Thompson (9)

St Patrick's Roman Catholic Primary School, Langley Moor

Slimey's Adventure

Slimey comes from Nailtor, the mystic land,
He lives in a hot heap of crumbly sand
He has five horn-like, sharpened spikes
He's going on an exciting hike
Everyone will be terrified of him,
Because of his gnarly, nasty grin
He soon arrived at the local play park,
No one was there because it was gloomy and dark
He curled up in a small ball,
In the morning, he went to a massive mall

Everyone quickly ran out,
With a loud scream and shout
He took some cheddar cheese,
And went back to the trees
He went in the dustbin for his last night,
He didn't want to give anyone else a ferocious
fright
In the morning, he went home,
To carry on his life alone.

Leo Currien (9)
St Patrick's Roman Catholic Primary School, Langley Moor

Dave The Baddy

I met a monster as huge as a whale,
White as snow and very pale
I saw that he had teeth that were shimmery and
shiny
And hair that was very slimy
Dave's eyes were bloodshot,
And his pupil was just one tiny, black dot

This creature's roar was as loud as a lion,
And I was sat there sighing
By the time it finished, I was dying
And the monster was using his last, little breath
And I thought I was about to meet my death

Dave was always angry and was always stomping,
And when he was happy, he was always doing
something
He always trod around the house like a little kid,
But I think that was good because he was always
opening the cookie jar lid.

Joanna Bull (9)
St Patrick's Roman Catholic Primary School, Langley Moor

About Dave The Fire Monster

My monster was from the core of the world,
If you had seen his brothers, you would have hurled
He had a rich smell of a flickering fire,
Steak was the food which he'd mostly desire
He had teeth as sharp as a knife,
His brothers and sisters had a short life

My monster had five electric blue eyes,
When we played hide-and-seek, he gave me five tries
The day came when I would meet,
My monster in a small, damp street
I think my monster is sleeping now,
So everyone, be quiet now!

Harris Armstrong (9)
St Patrick's Roman Catholic Primary School, Langley Moor

Rainybow The Rainbow Monster!

Rainybow is short and fat,
She loves to wear her top hat
It's made of felt, the colour is black,
It often hangs down her back

She lives on an island in the big, blue sea,
She always smiles and waves at me
She swims in the morning and again in the night,
If you saw her, you'd glimpse her bright light

You'd think she was happy, but no, she's sad
She has no friends to make her glad
Rainybow is short and fat,
She loves to wear her new top hat!

Ella Ellies (7)

St Patrick's Roman Catholic Primary School, Langley Moor

The Friendly Monster

Today, I met a monster, it came into my house,
It moved so quickly like a speedy mouse

It was so naughty as I chased it around,
Without making a single sound

When we arrived on a hill,
There were a lot of daffodils

He turned pale,
When there was a sea whale

We went back home,
And we were both alone

We then went to visit the Queen,
Then he turned green

He went back home,
As he met another friend, a gnome.

Belladouna Pulotu (8)
St Patrick's Roman Catholic Primary School, Langley Moor

Smelly Shep

Shep is an unknown species,
He has twelve slimy suckers
Smelly Shep is as ugly as a zombie,
Shep has a silly face but no muckers

Stupid Shep likes toasters,
The thing isn't very smart
He has lots of heaters,
Shep cannot eat tarts

I'd hope we'd not meet or I'd be mincemeat,
He doesn't know what conversation means
Annoying Shep cannot sit on any seat,
He doesn't eat any edamame beans.

Cassidy Philip Di Lella Edwards (9)
St Patrick's Roman Catholic Primary School, Langley Moor

The Monster Who Lives On An Island

Jendy is short and fat,
She loves her new top hat
It's made of felt, the colour is black,
It often hangs down her back

She lives on an island in the big sea,
Jendy always smiles and waves at me
She swims in the morning and night
If you see her, you will see the light!

She is always happy, not sad
She has lots of friends to make her glad
Jendy likes to fly,
She might be sitting on a bay.

Izabel Alex Bartlett (8)
St Patrick's Roman Catholic Primary School, Langley Moor

The Purple Monster

Purple loves Candy Land,
She is as fluffy as a furball
She is as naughty as a clown,
She is as happy as a horse
My monster has a bow,
On her purple toe
She looks nice,
But she is not as nice as a dice
She is as mean as a bad dragon
She went for a swim in the deep blue sea,
She saw a huge person, whose name was Cursten.
She said, "Hi."
But the monster didn't reply.

Kelsey Oakes (7)
St Patrick's Roman Catholic Primary School, Langley Moor

Fuzz

I met the monster from outer space,
Just after I won a race

The monster's name was Fuzz,
But some people called him Buzz

He decided to get an ice cream,
Fuzz turned from orange to blue and began to lean

I took Fuzz to school,
And everyone thought he was pretty cool

Soon, he decided to leave,
And so did the bees.

Robert Ellison (8)
St Patrick's Roman Catholic Primary School, Langley Moor

Scorps

I am the king of scorpions,
I am from Egypt
I have gooey, green warts
All over my face

I drink vile vermin smile,
Snakes and terrible tarantulas
I will kill everyone,
Who wants to battle

My pincers are as sharp as crocodile teeth
My skin is a large lizard
I live on meat,
Beware of me!

Ian Kenny (8)
St Patrick's Roman Catholic Primary School, Langley Moor

My Monster Sparky

My miniature monster, Sparky,
Was as slow as a tortoise
He liked to eat rice,
And sometimes chase mice
He liked to play with dice,
And sometimes, we played twice
When he was electrified,
He became petrified
Then one day, he got fried,
And he sadly died
But maybe one day, he will come alive.

Vaidotas Treciokas (8)
St Patrick's Roman Catholic Primary School, Langley Moor

Libby Long Neck And The Circus

Nelly the elephant woke one day,
And didn't know what on Earth to say
For there in front of circus Big Top,
Was a sight that made her eyes go *pop!*

The tallest thing with a neck so long,
It looked so different and quite wrong
"A monster!" cried poor Nelly loud,
But the creature looked all sad, head bowed

As our Nelly came more near,
She saw the monster cry a tear
"What are you?" questioned Nelly next,
But still no answer - she got vexed!

So next, she looked in a nature book,
For monsters with a long, necky look
And there it was, she had to laugh,
This monster was in fact a giraffe!

"I'll name you Libby Long Neck, mate,
Our circus is for love, not hate,
So don't be sad, you can stay here."
And that she did, with no more fear.

Martha McGrother (8)
Whitehouse Primary School, Elm Tree

My Big Scary Monster

My monster's eyes are as red as rubies glistening
in the sun,
His eyes are like burning coal, they're full of fury
My monster has blood dripping from his razor-
sharp spikes,
His spikes are as sharp as sharks' teeth!

My monster's body odour is revolting and vile,
He smells like garbage over 200 years old
He smells like putrid cheese that's out of date,
My monster is as stinky as rotten fish

My monster roars like a tremendous explosion,
He rattles your bones and his voice booms like
thunder,
When he whispers, it sounds like nails down a
blackboard

My monster is bloodthirsty and as deadly as the
plague,
He takes human bodies back to his tenebrous cave
and stores them

He is gruesome and mangy like a mouldy corpse,
He is as scary as your worst nightmare.

Talia Anne Lowe (9)
Whitehouse Primary School, Elm Tree

The Search For The Dark Shifter

Steps getting louder,
His breath becoming stronger
I can feel him near me,
But I cannot yet see
Through the woods I run,
Hoping to catch a glimpse of him,
Before the rise of the morning sun,
But my eyes are growing dim
I am looking under every rock,
I stare at all the trees
Then suddenly, I get a shock
He is there in front of me
I lay my trap,
I hold my breath
My heart is pounding,
I need him just to take one more step
I give him a smile,
And he starts to run

He's in the trap,
And I have won
As the sun starts to rise,
We can all now relax
As his body shrinks in size,
Everyone cheers, "The beast is gone!
He's the size of a pea,
Let's cook him for tea!"

James Angus Macdonald (9)
Whitehouse Primary School, Elm Tree

Monster Under My Bed

There was once a monster who lived under my bed,
He was small, round and fluffy with claws that
were red.

His eyes were bright yellow, and they sparkled in
the night,
But no matter how hard he tried, he could not give
me a fright!

I thought he was cute, but scary he was not!
In the end we became friends and at night we
talked a lot!

At bedtime he would appear,
We would stay up all night long, watch movies,
laugh and giggle, making our own cheer.

Then one day he stopped coming and I became so
sad.
I missed my red monster, the best friend I had.
The weeks went by slowly, I missed him more and
more.
I will never forget my best monster friend who left
me when I turned four!

Josie Mae Jolly (9)
Whitehouse Primary School, Elm Tree

Blobbins The Alien From Planet IT

Blobbins was born on Planet IT,
He is a slimy alien,
Blobbins doesn't have any fun, fantastic friends,
Blobbins' fangs are always growing greatly,
There was a jungle of various veiny black wires,
Blobbins wanted to go on an amazing adventure,
So one day Blobbins set off to the jungle
Of various veiny black wires,
Blobbins is a great gentle creature
So when he came to a grizzly bear
He just ran away!
He tried it again, fantastically fierce,
He did it!
He went back and told his patient parents,
They were so perfectly proud of him,
That was the end of Blobbins' amazing adventure.

Amy Louise Metcalf (8)
Whitehouse Primary School, Elm Tree

The Mysterious Monster

Darkness...
In the back of the corner of the room
A strange figure lay still
Breathing heavily and growling.

I was nervous
I didn't dare get out from my cosy bed
To go and turn on the light
To reveal the thing...
Knowing that I had to do this,
Slowly I crept on my tiptoes,
Step by step
Getting closer to the switch
It exposed the monster.

Click!
My eyes looked straight at the monster
By surprise, it was the cutest ball of fluff ever!
It was lying sound asleep
The monster Pinke Pie's fur was as soft as a cloud
And it was pink like candyfloss.

He was a giant teddy bear
Waiting for a hug off a girl like me!

Elizabeth Dalgleish (8)
Whitehouse Primary School, Elm Tree

The Monsters In The Wardrobe

The monsters in my wardrobe,
Like to sleep the day away
So when I get home from school,
I let them out to play

When mum calls me for supper,
I give them a broom
First they tidy my toys,
And then the whole room

The mummy hates to vacuum,
So if she starts to whine
I kick her in the butt and say,
"Swap jobs with Frankenstein!"

When the room is nice and neat,
I bring them out some food
When Dracula wants to drink my blood,
I think it's pretty rude!

I've cared for them
For as long as I can recall
The monsters in the wardrobe,
Are the nicest ones of all.

Elif Tiffany (9)
Whitehouse Primary School, Elm Tree

Giant James

The monster is tall and big,
Like a giraffe
But even if you're small,
He will make you laugh

The monster is from Stockton-on-Tees,
And the monster goes to Wembley,
Let's win, please!

He has no friends,
But that's all good
Because he has a great family,
Like everyone should

He is fierce,
Like he has tears
He can sometimes be sad,
But he is never mad

Giant James would make the best friend,
Because he would always be there for you right till
the end.

Joey Saysell (7)
Whitehouse Primary School, Elm Tree

The Friendly Monster

F ive days he walks down the street
I ce cream for a treat
V enison, meat he doesn't like to eat
E legant is the way he dresses

E normous feet stomping is angry
Y o-yo going up and down
E ggshells, he likes to beat
D oughnut-shaped ears

H e likes to see the ocean
A ll around him, there are many people
K ath is his mum's name
E yes like a lion
E ggy is his middle name
M ad like a gorilla.

Hakeem Khan (8)
Whitehouse Primary School, Elm Tree

Fluffball And The Lost Ball

Fluffball was never tall,
He loved to play with the ball
He was the kindest monster of them all,
But then one day, his friends came to call
The ball was lost, he couldn't find it at all,
His friends felt bad, they searched and searched
They even looked behind the church
All was well in the end,
Fluffball's very special friend
Spied the ball in Fluffball's hair,
No one could find it there
The monsters all enjoyed their play,
They all came back the very next day.

Joseph Canvin-Reid (8)
Whitehouse Primary School, Elm Tree

Monsters!

There are lots of monsters,
There are fluffy monsters,
There are scary monsters,
There are cute monsters
And there are greedy monsters

But my monster is special,
He has glowing spots
And pointy wings
He has four legs,
And has six eyes

His horns have neon colours,
He is special because he is himself

I love all monsters but mine is special,
He lives on Mars and he has a friend called Macie,
My monster's special because I love him.

Alice Potter (9)
Whitehouse Primary School, Elm Tree

The Rise Of Shadow Shifter

Lurking in the shadows is the Shadow Shifter,
His eyes glow yellow like flames
He lives inside a gigantic volcano in complete
isolation,
He arose from the flames, it first erupted centuries
ago
For years and years, he stayed out of sight,
Perfecting his skills so he can hunt and fight
Over time, he gained power,
Growing stronger, hour by hour
His shape changes form at his will,
One day a dragon,
One day a beast,
One day a giant,
Now he can feast.

Mohammedadeen Yousaf (9)
Whitehouse Primary School, Elm Tree

Ed Under My Bed

There is a monster called Ed,
He hides under my bed.
He's got a very, very big nose,
He likes to tickle my toes.
He's very big and scary,
His toes are long and hairy.
He sometimes watches telly,
And sits and rubs his belly.
He likes to sit and pump,
He smells like a dump.
He's got scary, red eyes,
And he likes to eat pies.
He comes from a place,
Far out in space.
He sleeps in a box,
And steals all my socks.

Jack Lewis Dunham (9)
Whitehouse Primary School, Elm Tree

My Friendly, Fishy Monster

I know a friendly monster called Sammy,
He lives in a cave under the sea.
He has a scaly body,
And five golden eyes to see.

If I stand above the water,
I can see him staring at me.
He has six orange arms that look like crab claws,
For him to catch his tea.

A colourful fish tail so he can swim.
He plays in and out of the water,
Gleaming in the sea.
He is my friendly fishy monster,
I wish I could play and swim with him.

Maggie May George (9)
Whitehouse Primary School, Elm Tree

The Peculiar Visitor

It was just a normal day,
And I was going out to play
When there was a mysterious knock at the door,
Which was followed by a loud roar

As I went to see who it was,
I could easily tell because
The visitor was as grumpy as could be,
And I could tell it was a 'he'

He looked at me and gave me a smile,
I'd been waiting for a while
As we got into the car,
He asked me, "Are we going far?"

Poppi-Lei Brooks (9)
Whitehouse Primary School, Elm Tree

Shapety On A Bow Hunt

(Haiku poetry)

Her name is Shapety,
She was a nice, kind monster
She was also mean

She has cleverness,
Monsters say she is stinky,
And sometimes ugly

She's a shape-shifter,
Which means she's really naughty
She wants to travel

Shapety lost her bow,
It went into Monston City,
She grabbed her best friends

They ran where it went,
Her friend, Jo, had got the bow
Shapety was so pleased.

Hollie Brennan (9)
Whitehouse Primary School, Elm Tree

Lefty Leave

It came from a mountain,
It's rather green and white
Its face is like the tip of a mountain
The bottom is like grass,
Its name is Lefty Leave

Lefty Leave, Lefty Leave,
He is on the loose
We need volunteers,
If you catch him,
The reward is rich

One eye,
A couple of legs
No one will know the truth
Even if you see him,
He will get mad,
Lefty Leave, Lefty Leave, we need help.

Amy May Jackson (9)
Whitehouse Primary School, Elm Tree

Back-To-Back With Jack And Zack

There's a cute, little monster named Jack,
Who has a problem on his back
Where his beastly brother Zack is attached

Zack is grumpy and always gets in trouble for
being loud,
Jack is friendly and polite but this can cause them
to fight
Especially at night, when Zack steals the cover and
pulls it tight

But deep down, they are close and care for each
other,
When they say, "Goodnight, brother."

Jack Dalzell (8)
Whitehouse Primary School, Elm Tree

My Monster

My monster's name is Snuggles,
And he loves a lot of cuddles,
He is very funny,
He really loves his mummy,
When he was little,
He was as naughty as a monkey,
And also, he smelt a bit funky,
Snuggles is from an enchanted land,
That is shaped like a hand,
Snuggles loves to travel all over,
To find a four-leaf clover,
His wings are as big as a lion,
But he doesn't do crying!

Millie Rafferty (9)
Whitehouse Primary School, Elm Tree

The Tall And Friendly Monster

I know of a friendly monster,
He lives in the woods all tall and fat
He seems to eat all day which can't be good,
He only comes out at night
He rummages through our bins,
But keeps out of sight
I saw him once, he seemed nice
He is as orange as a Wotsit and has black spots just like a dice
He does not have any teeth but smells a lot,
I know of a friendly monster.

Elias Sturman (9)
Whitehouse Primary School, Elm Tree

Mary Mango Monster

Mary Mango Monster,
She lives up in a tree

She only comes down,
At half-past three

Her best friend is an alien,
From a planet far, far away

That is why Mary Mango Monster,
Never goes out to play

When she comes for tea,
Her mammy serves them mango

And when they finish their food
They both dance the tango!

Lillia Grace Tucker (9)
Whitehouse Primary School, Elm Tree

Dragon

The fire was like a hot volcano,
Red like the sun,
Suddenly, the volcano erupted,
Red-hot lava everywhere,
But the dragon didn't think he would be brave.
He jumped over the volcano
And saved a kitten,
The kitten was so glad to be alive,
It let out an enormous miaow!

Tilly the dragon and Ruby the kitten
Were friends forever.

Ruby Atkinson (8)
Whitehouse Primary School, Elm Tree

Stitch!

Stitch is a friendly cat,
He's half-cat, half-lizard
He likes to wear different hats,
He is some kind of wizard!
He is really weird,
He wouldn't like to have a beard
He would like to go to the moon,
But he said it too soon!
He likes to eat pasta,
He wouldn't like to be a gangster,
This is Stitch,
He isn't a witch!

Elena Rurzman (9)
Whitehouse Primary School, Elm Tree

Ice Pops The Cyclops

Ice Pops lives in my shed,
She has spots, and purple hair
And one massive eye to stare
She only comes out at night,
Staring at the cats and giving them a fright,
And making them fight

I went in the shed to play,
She was crying, it made me sad
I told her she was pretty,
Even with one eye,
So we carried on playing I spy.

Connie Manning (9)
Whitehouse Primary School, Elm Tree

Where, Where, Everywhere

Where, where, everywhere,
Are there no friends for me?
Is it my ugliness?
Is it my six eyes?
Only a friend will overtake my sighs!

Where, where, everywhere
Except for one place,
Called Earth?

Is it there,
Where I'll meet my destiny
Of a friend?
Well,
I'll have to wait,
And see!

Isobel Southall (9)
Whitehouse Primary School, Elm Tree

The Quest To Save Wereworld

Once, in a galaxy far, far away,
Lived a monster called Zap and his friend called
Zay
Zap was huge, daring and brave,
And had to save Wereworld from evil Dave
Dave was so scary, but Zap was so clever,
He put Dave in prison forever and ever
Wereworld was so peaceful and free,
Zap was made king, and what a king he will be!

Taylor Camilleri (9)
Whitehouse Primary School, Elm Tree

Milton The Monster

On Planet Zog,
Far, far away
There lives a monster named Milton,
Milton flies ships,
And explores space

Milton is helpful,
And has a lot of friends
He has twelve eyes and three heads,
Three legs, four arms,
He also has three hearts and is round and purple
Milton never comes out at night.

Daniel Harris (9)
Whitehouse Primary School, Elm Tree

The Monster With No Friends

Ellio, my monster, was from outer space,
He travelled to Earth from a faraway place,
He had no friends so he came down to Earth,
And landed in Australia, near Perth,
His skin was green and he had big teeth,
People were scared, their beds they hid
underneath,
Ellio was sad and he had no one to play with.

Elliott Godfrey (9)
Whitehouse Primary School, Elm Tree

Catider

Fluff was a catider,
A catider is a cat and spider mixed together
Fluff went to the sweet shop,
At the door, she had to stop
She bought M&M's,
She bought cherry Maoam sweets
She went home with the sweets,
Fluff snuggled on the sofa with her family,
And ate the sweets.

Freja Carlsson (8)
Whitehouse Primary School, Elm Tree

Release The Beast

This is no ordinary monster,
This is a beast
A beast from the North East
Floating in the water
It waits for its prey
Because it will not stay
With its green, scaly skin,
And big, blue, beady eyes
It sees its prey from afar,
If nothing else, it will leave a scar.

JJ Hardy (9)
Whitehouse Primary School, Elm Tree

My Poor Monster Zog

Zog, Zog, oh dear Zog!
Why couldn't you be,
A fantastic monster like me?

You have feet as big as a yeti,
Why wouldn't you be, a fantastic monster like me?

You're as loud as an exploding volcano!
Why shouldn't you be a fantastic monster like me?

Jake Cinnamond (8)
Whitehouse Primary School, Elm Tree

There Once Was A Weird Monster

There was a monster from France,
Who didn't like to dance
He was very crazy,
But also lazy
He was small, pretty and pink,
But never liked to think
He was very shy,
He'd never cry
If you played with him, his games were fun,
He was tired of the sun.

Chelsea Shipman (8)
Whitehouse Primary School, Elm Tree

Bloby

Bloby is a shy, scared monster,
He is flat and gooey
He can take the shape of anything,
Although it can be a bit pooey

His antennae can sense anything,
His talons are scary
His snout is big,
But his fangs are filled with dairy.

Matthew Longfield (9)
Whitehouse Primary School, Elm Tree

Bob The Friendly Monster!

Bob the friendly monster,
Is very gentle,
But when he's being naughty,
He drives me mental

Bob is very fluffy,
Which makes him stinky and stuffy
Bob lives on Stuff Land,
With lots more monsters that all get out of hand.

Eleanor Lowe (8)
Whitehouse Primary School, Elm Tree

Keith

There once was a monster called Keith,
And he had very long teeth
His arms were long and were very strong
He was as big as King Kong,
The horns on his head were as heavy as lead
And often got stuck on the bed!

James Wood (8)
Whitehouse Primary School, Elm Tree

Under The Bed

What's that under your bed?
It is the slimy dragon
It will never leave.
For a bedtime snack,
Watch out,
It might be you!

Always check under your bed,
The dragon might eat you!

Matthew Teague (9)
Whitehouse Primary School, Elm Tree

My Rainbow Friend

I have a rainbow, furry friend
She's very colourful
She's very friendly
Her name is Kirby
To others, she looks scary
To me, she's my best friend
My rainbow, furry friend, Kirby.

Tegan Henry (8)
Whitehouse Primary School, Elm Tree

Bubbles

Bubbles, the blue, bubbly monster, is very fantastic,
His cute face is a furry place,
Bubbles likes to shrink and wink,
Blue Bubbles loves cuddles,
My cuddles find Bubbles.

Poppy McEwan (8)
Whitehouse Primary School, Elm Tree

Trixy

T is for terrifying

R is for raging

I is for infuriating

X if for X-ray

Y is for yikes (when people see her!)

Elisha Kingston (7)

Whitehouse Primary School, Elm Tree

YOUNG WRITERS INFORMATION

We hope you have enjoyed reading this book – and that you will continue to in the coming years.

If you're a young writer who enjoys reading and creative writing, or the parent of an enthusiastic poet or story writer, do visit our website **www.youngwriters.co.uk**. Here you will find free competitions, workshops and games, as well as recommended reads, a poetry glossary and our blog.

If you would like to order further copies of this book, or any of our other titles, then please give us a call or visit **www.youngwriters.co.uk**.

Young Writers
Remus House
Coltsfoot Drive
Peterborough
PE2 9BF
(01733) 890066
info@youngwriters.co.uk